I AM
HOUSTON

By
Mary Dodson Wade

Illustrated by
Pat Finney

COLOPHON HOUSE   HOUSTON, TEXAS

Cataloging-in-Publication Data

Wade, Mary Dodson
I Am Houston / by Mary Dodson Wade.
  p. cm.

Summary: A biography of the famous general, politician, and friend
of Indians. It follows his life in Tennessee and Washington, D.C.
and details his adventures in shaping both the Republic and the
state of Texas.
1. Houston, Sam, 1793-1863—Juvenile literature. 2. Texas—
History—Juvenile Literature. [1. Houston, Sam 2. Texas—History]
I. Title
ISBN 1-882539-05-2
ISBN 1-882539-06-0 (pbk)
F390.H84W33   1993
976.4092
[B]

In memory of my father.
Like Sam Houston, he was a large man
who planted his feet,
and you never had to ask him where he stood.

*C*aptain *Samuel Houston* urged his horse homeward to Timber Ridge Plantation. He reached his two-story house in Rockbridge County, Virginia, just a few days before the birth of his fifth son. When the healthy boy arrived on March 2, 1793, Captain Houston gave this son his own name.

In the next few years, another son and three daughters joined young Sam Houston and his older brothers. Their father, an army officer, was gone for long periods of time, and Elizabeth Paxton Houston raised the children and managed the plantation.

Sam was tall for his age. His father had given land for a school, but Sam didn't like to go. There were times, however, when he would leave whatever he was doing and run to the schoolhouse so that he could take part in the spelling bee. He preferred to stretch out by himself and read books from his father's library, especially his favorite—*The Iliad,* a book about ancient Greek heroes.

By the time Sam was fourteen, however, Captain Houston was dead and their money was gone. Elizabeth Houston sold Timber Ridge. She packed her nine children and all their belongings in two wagons and drove to east Tennessee. They settled there on land Captain Houston had chosen before he died.

Once they reached Marysville in Blount County, the Houstons went to work — all except Sam. The tall, good-looking lad with wavy brown hair and piercing blue eyes kept reading. His older brothers said he should work in the store. Sam disappeared into the forest.

Before long, word came that he was living with the Cherokee Indians beyond the Tennessee River. The older brothers went to get him, but Sam balked. "I prefer measuring deer tracks to measuring tape," he said, and his brothers left him there.

Life with the Indians suited Sam perfectly. Chief Oo-loo-te-ka, head of a peaceful Cherokee tribe, adopted him and gave Sam the Indian name Co-lon-neh. It meant The Raven.

The Raven played with Cherokee friends, mastered their games and skills, and even began to think like an Indian. He also had his books and read *The Iliad* so often that he could quote most of it. Best of all, no one told him what to do.

For three years he lived as a Cherokee. He adopted the Indian custom of talking about himself as if he were someone else. When he was old, Sam Houston said, "Houston has seen almost all there is to see of life, but nothing is so sweet to remember as those days with the children of the forest."

At the age of nineteen, however, Sam left

this carefree life and went back to Marysville. He needed to pay for things he had bought at the store when he had come home on short visits.

People scoffed when he announced he was going to be a teacher. He had never gone to school. But Sam had read more books than anyone else, and he was the best speller in the county. He could quote long poems, especially his beloved *Iliad*.

The fee for his school was twice as much as what other teachers charged, and he was specific about how it was to be paid. "One-third of my salary is to be paid in cash, one-third in corn for me and my horse, and one-third in bright calico cloth for shirts." It wasn't long before he was standing before a completely filled room.

Well over six feet tall, the teacher had no trouble with his students. His wavy brown hair hung in a queue down the back of his calico shirts. In his hand was a blue and white sourwood stick he had made by peeling the bark in a spiral and then placing the stick in the fire.

The future general was happy with his first command, and his signature matched his colorful shirts. He boldly made the letters and then put many swirls and scrolls under it. With the "S" separated from the other letters of his first name, it seemed to say "I am Houston."

*I*n *1813, the United States* was at war with England again. Sam was barely twenty years old.

One day, soldiers in white pantaloons and smart waistcoats marched into Marysville looking for volunteers. Sam had seen militia volunteers dressed in homespun outfits, but this was different.

He stepped forward and picked up the silver dollar off the drum. With that, he became a soldier in the regular army, just as his father had been.

As he left, Elizabeth Houston gave her son a gun and slipped a ring on his finger. "My door is always open to brave men," she said, "but it is eternally shut against cowards."

Sam was a natural leader. He did well in the army and in just a few months had become head of an infantry platoon.

Before long, the American soldiers were sent to Alabama, but they were not facing the British army. They were sent to fight the Creek Indians who had sided with the British.

General Andrew Jackson was in command. He meant to clear out the Creeks so that he could concentrate on fighting the British.

During the fierce battle at Horseshoe Bend, Sam lead a charge against the Creeks. Suddenly a barbed arrow struck him in the leg. He stopped a soldier and ordered him to pull it out. The soldier pulled with all his might, and Sam was left with a great gash on his leg.

General Jackson rode by and ordered the wounded soldier to stay behind the lines, but Sam did not obey. When the call came to storm the fort where the Creeks were, he dashed out.

As he raced alone toward the fort, a bullet shattered his arm and shoulder. He stumbled back to safety.

The general saw the young officer's courage, but the army doctors did not even bother to treat his wounds. They thought he would die before morning.

The other wounded soldiers were taken for treatment, but Sam went two months without proper medicine. When he returned to his mother's house, he was so gaunt that she recognized him only by his eyes.

Sam stayed in the army. Doctors operated to remove the bullet in his shoulder, but the wound never completely healed.

Not long afterwards, he was appointed Indian agent because he knew the Indians so well. He ordered pots for the women and traps for the hunters. He got supplies and blankets for them. He also urged the Cherokees to keep the treaty they had signed saying they would move farther west.

The Cherokees did not want to go. To them, the West was a place of destruction and death. Proof of this seemed to come when one of the chiefs returned from there with news that his people were starving.

Sam accompanied the chief to Washington to talk to the government about the food and supplies that had been promised. The Secretary of War was outraged to see Sam dressed like a Cherokee. He sternly reprimanded the young lieutenant for being out of uniform.

Then the Secretary accused him of stealing from the Indians. Sam immediately proved who the guilty ones were, but no one was punished.

Furious, he wrote an angry letter resigning from the army. That unusual "S" made it seem to say "I am Houston."

*S*am *Houston,* twenty-five-years-old and in debt, went to Nashville, Tennessee. A lawyer there gave him books to read. "It will take eighteen months for you to know enough to be a lawyer," he said. Six months later Houston passed the state examination.

He moved to Lebanon, thirty miles east of Nashville, to begin his practice. A merchant rented him an office for a dollar a month and gave him clothes. The tall, handsome lawyer in tight breeches, colorful vest, plum-colored coat, and beaver hat caught everyone's attention. He

charmed the ladies with his courteous manners. Men listened and argued his views about politics and how to run the government.

On his many trips to Nashville, Houston always stopped at the Hermitage, Andrew Jackson's big plantation home. The Jacksons treated Houston like a son, and the young lawyer considered himself part of their family. He admired the powerful Tennessee politician and often sent presents to Rachel Jackson. When she died, he led the pall bearers at her funeral.

With Jackson's help, Houston soon became head of the state militia. Before long, his success as a trial lawyer led to the job of state attorney general.

Then, in 1823, he was elected congress-man from Tennessee. This time, he walked the streets of Washington dressed as a fashionable gentleman.

Four years later, the dashing congressman left Washington to became governor of Tennessee. He was so popular that there was talk of his running for president.

It seemed just one more happy event when he married Eliza Allen on January 29, 1829. She was eighteen; he was thirty-five. Eliza's family was wealthy and prominent, a great help for anyone in public office. And what a catch the handsome governor was!

Then, less than three months after their marriage, Eliza left her husband and returned to her father's house. The governor's enemies immediately spread ugly rumors about him and said that he had mistreated Eliza.

Houston's friends urged him to defend himself, but he sealed his lips and dared any one to speak ill of Eliza.

To his death, he kept that silence. "It is no part of a gentleman to make war against a woman," he said. "If my character cannot stand the shock, then let me lose it."

It was not his character, however, that suffered. It was his career. On April 16, 1829, he sat in his room near the Tennessee capitol building. Slowly, he shaved the end of an eagle feather into a pen. Then he dipped it into the ink and began to write.

He struggled with the words, crossing them out again and again. Finally, at the end of the long letter, he wrote, "It has become my duty to resign as governor."

At the bottom he signed in the familiar script.

A week later, Houston boarded a steamer to leave Tennessee. At that moment an eagle flew overhead. It screamed and then disappeared into the sunset. It was a sign any Indian would recognize. "My destiny is in the West," he said.

Before many weeks, he reached the Cherokee Nation. Chief Oo-loo-te-ka welcomed him to his home among the cottonwood trees on the Arkansas River. "My son," said the Raven's adopted father, "eleven winters have passed since we last met. I have heard that you were a

great chief among your people. Now we need help, and the Great Spirit has sent you to us. My wigwam is yours."

The Raven slipped easily into Indian life. He attended councils dressed in a beaded white doeskin shirt and long yellow leggings. On his head he wore feathers or a colorful silk turban. He became spokesman for a number of other tribes, and the Cherokees declared him their full-blood brother.

A year after leaving Tennessee, the Raven returned to Washington. He had a bright blanket thrown over his shoulders. Metal ornaments tinkled as he walked. He brought Indian complaints to his friend, President Andrew Jackson. Jackson listened and removed many of the agents.

Soon after returning to Oo-loo-te-ka's home, he built a large house on the Neosho River and took Tiana Rogers, a Cherokee widow, as his wife.

But dark days came for the Raven. For months he did nothing but drink whiskey. He no longer spoke at councils, and the Indians gave him a new name — "Big Drunk."

No one seemed to need or want the man who had once so proudly signed his name with the peculiar "S."

In the fall of 1831, things changed. Houston sped to Tennessee for a last visit with his mother. The death of this woman he admired stirred him to action.

Soon he was back in Washington speaking for his Indian friends. He wore a buckskin coat with beaver collar, the gift of an Indian chief. A hunting knife hung at his belt, and he carried a cane which he had carved when he and the Cherokees had stopped at the Hermitage.

While in Washington, Houston became involved in a brawl. Congressman William

Stanbery accused him of dishonesty in dealing with the Indians. Houston exploded and challenged the congressman to a duel. Stanbery refused but started carrying a gun.

One day the two large men met on the street. Houston began to beat Stanbery with his cane. The congressman tried to shoot Houston, but his gun didn't fire.

The sensational affair was the talk of Washington. Stanbery insisted that Houston be tried by Congress. Jackson worried that his favorite might lose. "Buck up your defense," he ordered. Then he threw some money on the table. "Get yourself some new clothes."

The day of the trial, every seat in Congress was filled. Dressed in stylish waist coat, matching trousers, and white satin vest, Houston made an eloquent speech. Congress found him guilty anyway.

The Speaker of the House, however, made short work of the punishment. "I am to censure you," he said, "and by this statement have done so." Houston never had to pay the fine.

The whole affair brought him back into

politics. He gave Tiana the big house and never returned to live with the Indians. He had found a new mission—to fill Andrew Jackson's wish to bring Texas into the union.

On December 1, 1832, he crossed the Red River into Texas, which was part of Mexico. His passport from the United States requested safe passage for "General Samuel Houston, a citizen of the United States, thirty-eight years of age, six feet two inches in stature, brown hair and light complexion."

In a sweeping tour, he went first to Nacogdoches, then to San Felipe de Austin. Stephen Austin, the man who had brought the American settlers to Texas, was away from his seat of government. Instead, Houston ate Christmas dinner with red-headed Jim Bowie.

The two rode together to San Antonio de Bexar. Bowie introduced Houston to his father-in-law, vice-governor of the Spanish province Don Juan Veramendi. Sam Houston charmed the vice-governor's wife.

Soon he crossed back into Louisiana and wrote Jackson a glowing report. It said what the president wanted to hear. "The citizens of Texas favor joining the United States twenty to one. I believe they will form a state government, and I expect to attend the convention to write the constitution. I may make Texas my abiding place."

At the bottom was his usual signature.

*S*am *Houston attended* the convention in 1833. It adopted a constitution making Texas a separate Mexican state. He declared the constitution "one of the best in existence." He had written most of it.

After Stephen Austin left to present the constitution to the Mexican government, Houston returned to Nacogdoches. He began practicing law and entered into the town's social life. As usual, he won the hearts of the ladies.

Houston lived with Alcalde (Mayor) Adolphus Sterne. Because Mexico required all settlers to join the Catholic church, Mrs. Sterne became his god-mother. He called her "Madre Mio" and gave her presents.

In Nacogdoches, Houston met seventeen-year-old Anna Raguet. This well-educated young lady began to teach Spanish to the handsome lawyer, and he began to court her.

Stephen Austin, in the meantime, had been jailed in Mexico soon after delivering the Texas constitution. Angry Texans now demanded complete freedom. After two years of imprisonment, Austin returned. "War is the only way," said the quiet leader.

Anna tied a sash on Sam Houston's sword and sent him off. Soon he was elected commander-in-chief of the army.

His orders, however, were ignored by other officers. Houston knew he must have trained soldiers and obedient officers in order to meet the highly professional Mexican army. But no one expected Mexican dictator Antonio López de Santa Anna to march north any time soon.

Houston sent Bowie, whom he trusted, to

San Antonio. The Alamo had been stripped of supplies, and Houston felt it should be abandoned.

Suddenly, Santa Anna's army appeared. Late February, while the Texans were trying to organize a government at Washington-on-the-Brazos, a letter arrived from William Barrett Travis. The commander at the Alamo wrote, "I am besieged by a thousand or more Mexicans under Santa Anna. I SHALL NEVER SURRENDER OR RETREAT. Come to our aid. I shall sustain myself as along as possible. VICTORY OR DEATH!"

Delegates worked through the night in a cold, unfinished building to complete the Texas Declaration of Independence.

On March 2, 1836, Houston celebrated his forty-fourth birthday by sending "Madre Mio" a beautiful pair of two-inch-long earrings. He asked her to wear them every year to honor his birthday and that of Texas. Eva Rosine Sterne faithfully followed his request. Fifty years later, she wore the earrings for the last time at the dedication of the state capitol building in Austin.

That same March 2, 1836, he put his bold "I am Houston" on the document that made Texas a free country.

*F*our *days later,* on March 6, a rider reached Washington-on-the-Brazos with the last, desperate letter from the Alamo defenders. The convention delegates scrambled to the door to go to their aid. Houston called them back because Texas needed to form a government if it hoped to win its freedom.

It was the commander-in-chief, wearing a Cherokee coat, buckskin vest, and broad-brimmed hat, who galloped away. The tall figure and his four companions headed for San Antonio 175 miles west.

Early the next morning, Houston walked a little distance from the others and listened intently. "The bombardment has stopped," he said. "I fear the Alamo has fallen."

At Gonzales they found 374 men gathered. Houston had just formed them into army units when a Mexican rider raced into town with news that the Alamo had fallen.

Houston sent scout Deaf Smith to check the story. Smith soon returned with Susannah Dickenson, her little girl, and William Travis's servant Joe. They confirmed the dreadful story. Travis, Bowie, David Crockett—all 185 defenders of the Alamo were dead.

The commander-in-chief ordered everything they could not carry to be destroyed. He sent word for Colonel James Fannin and his 500 men to meet him at the Colorado River.

Terrified citizens fled eastward with the soldiers. Only once did they stop. Houston sent fifty men back to get a blind widow and her children who had been left behind.

Soon word came that Fannin and his men had been executed at Goliad. With his own troops deserting, Houston talked to no one. He ordered retreat again. In the rain, they crossed the Colorado River.

Again retreat. The men were force-marched to the flooded Brazos River.

Unable to get across, Houston drilled his soldiers, but there was no order to stand and fight.

Sitting in safety far away, temporary Texas president David G. Burnet ranted, "Sir: the enemy is laughing you to scorn. You must fight."

Still, Sam Houston issued no battle orders. "Coward!" grumbled the weary men as they watched the hunched figure whittling in his tent. If he planned to retreat until the Mexican army was far ahead of its supplies, he told no one. "If I err, the blame is mine," he said.

Both armies finally crossed the flooded Brazos. The Texans approached a fork in the road where the settlers would take a road to safety in the United States. The other led to Harrisburg and battle with Santa Anna. Rain-soaked soldiers, eager to fight and go home, cheered orders to march toward Harrisburg.

Mrs. Pamela Mann, however, pulled a gun and demanded her oxen that had been hauling two cannons. General Houston ordered the oxen unhitched and force-marched his soldiers across the boggy prairie. No more retreat. They would meet Santa Anna's troops.

The Texans won the race to San Jacinto. Houston positioned his men in the woods on a knoll near Lynchburg Ferry, and they watched Mexican troops cross for battle. Deaf Smith was sent to burn the bridge to prevent any retreat.

"Hold your fire," ordered Houston. He alone would signal the attack. Then he waited. Santa Anna did not know the patient stalking Sam Houston had learned from the Indians.

The next afternoon, April 21, 1836, the Mexican army stacked their guns and rested. Then, at 3:30 p.m., mounted on a magnificent white horse he had bought in Sugar Land, the Texas commander raised his sword. The Texans raced forward shouting, "Remember the Alamo! Remember Goliad!" They completely overran the unsuspecting Mexicans.

During the eighteen-minute battle, the

white stallion was shot. The wound in Houston's ankle filled his boot with blood, but he directed the battle from another horse.

In the end, nine Texans died and thirty more were wounded. Mexican losses were over 1300 dead, wounded, or captured.

Houston collapsed and was laid under an oak tree. While a doctor treated his shattered ankle, he arranged three magnolia leaves and wrote a note to Anna Raguet in Nacogdoches. "These are laurels I send you from the battle field of San Jacinto. Thine, Houston."

*I*n *all the confusion,* the Mexican commander had tried to escape. Santa Anna changed out of his uniform, but his own men gave him away. He demanded to be taken to Houston.

The victorious general, lying under the tree, offered the conquered one a box to sit on. "You are no common man," said Santa Anna. "You have conquered the Napoleon of the West."

Immediately, shouts went up to execute Santa Anna, but Houston refused. Texas could bargain for freedom if the Mexican dictator were alive.

Soon, Texas's straight-laced temporary president arrived at the battlefield. Burnet disliked Houston so much that he refused to let the wounded general board his steamer to get treatment for his worsening wound. The ship's captain, however, would not sail without the hero of San Jacinto.

After reaching Galveston, Burnet refused to allow Houston on board a Texas ship bound for New Orleans. The general, more dead than alive, sailed on a private schooner to get medical treatment.

When he returned two months later, people had not forgotten the battle at San Jacinto. Houston was overwhelmingly elected the first president of the Republic of Texas. He laid his sword on the table and took the oath of office.

The new capital city, named Houston in his honor, sported mud streets and log buildings. An often-drunk president slept on a cot in one room of a two-room cabin.

His biggest concern was invasion from Mexico. Three secretaries took dictation as he wrote letters seeking recognition of his new country. "In the name of the Republic of Texas, free, sovereign and independent. I, Sam Houston, send greetings." At the bottom he put the familiar signature.

The president of the Republic of Texas could not hold office two successive terms. Not one to go quietly, Sam Houston gave a rousing four-hour farewell speech before leaving.

With time to travel, he headed east. In Alabama, he stopped to buy horses, but it was beautiful Margaret Moffett Lea's violet eyes that captured his attention. By the time he left, she had promised to marry him.

When asked why a talented young woman of twenty would marry a man forty-seven years old, she answered simply, "He won my heart."

Houston's divorce from Eliza Allen was final, Tiana Rogers had died of pneumonia, and Anna Raguet would soon marry his friend Robert Irion.

Returning to Texas, he eagerly awaited Margaret's coming. Instead, her mother stepped off the boat. "General Houston," said Nancy Lea, "the man who takes my daughter's hand in marriage will do it in my home and not elsewhere."

Houston admired this woman of strong will and convictions. He traveled to Alabama, where he and Margaret were married on May 9, 1840.

He took his bride to a large house at Cedar Point on Galveston Bay. His friends predicted that the marriage wouldn't last six months. But Margaret's gentle ways and educated mind transformed the man known for his hard drinking and rough language.

In the meantime, Texas president Mirabeau Lamar had printed so much money for his grand plans that it became worthless. Then, to spite Houston, he moved the capital to Austin. Worst of all, an effort to clear Indians from

Texas caused the death of Houston's Cherokee friend, Chief Bowl. In an angry speech, Houston called the chief a better man than his murderers.

At the next election, 1842, Houston was back as president. He moved the capital to Washington-on-the-Brazos. Margaret joined him, and he made sure his talented wife had her rosewood piano. There, in May 1843 their first child, Sam Jr., was born.

Just a few months before the birth of his own son, he had written to Flaco, a famous Lipan Indian chief. The old warrior's son had died. "My heart is sad," Houston wrote. "A dark cloud rests upon your nation. The song of birds is silent. Grass shall not grow in the path between us. Thy brother, Houston."

*B*y *enforcing a strict budget,* Houston restored value to Texas money.

Then, hearing that Jackson was near death, the family raced to Tennessee. Houston wanted to tell his friend that Texas was finally going to be part of the United States. They arrived three hours too late, and Houston wept beside Jackson's bed.

On February 19, 1846, the flag of the Republic of Texas was lowered for the last time. Sam Houston caught its folds. Instead of retiring, however, he left almost immediately for

Washington and took his place as senator from the twenty-eighth state of the United States.

For the next thirteen years he spent long months away from home. Again, people talked of his being president. Not even illness slowed his busy schedule. People waiting to see him lined up in chairs leading to his bedside.

He missed his family and filled his letters with advice to the ever-increasing children. The oldest girl, Nancy Elizabeth, was named for her grandmothers. By the time she was six and a half, Nannie was reading the letters her father wrote her.

Sam Jr. had three other sisters. Maggie (Margaret Lea) was named for her mother. Red-headed Mary William was called Mollie. Nettie was named for her aunt, Antoinette Power.

"Poor Sam," wrote their father. "He is not getting the six brothers he ordered." When a little brother finally arrived, it was rambunctious Andrew Jackson.

Sam Houston was a well-known figure in

Washington. Sometimes he appeared with a Mexican blanket thrown over his shoulder and a sombrero on his head. At other times he wore a military cap and a short blue cloak with a bright red lining.

On Sundays he went to church. During the sermon, he carved wooden figures which he gave to children. In the afternoon he wrote Margaret long letters about the sermon.

Margaret, who suffered from asthma, answered faithfully. The family spent most of the time in Huntsville. Their plantation, Raven Hill, was several miles out in the country, but the house in town had a dog-run to catch the breeze. A separate log building allowed Houston to work in peace when he was home.

Sometimes, Joshua, the slave who took care of the property, hitched four horses to the big yellow coach. Then, coachman Tom Blue would drive the family to Cedar Point.

One day while Houston was in Huntsville, he saw a frightened slave child standing in the sun on the auction block. Jeff Hamilton was being sold to pay a liquor debt. Houston told the storekeeper to put the amount on his bill. He bought Jeff some candy and said, "I have a boy about your age."

Soon afterward, the Houstons bought a fourth house. This one was in Independence, a town with fine schools. Margaret's mother was a staunch member of the Baptist church there.

Then, in 1854, Margaret's work was complete. Sam Houston joined the church. He even pledged to pay half the minister's salary.

When he was baptized in Rocky Creek, someone asked if his sins were washed away. Houston chuckled. "I hope so, but if they are, the Lord help those fish down below."

Slavery was the central issue in Congress. Houston owned slaves, but his votes brought bitter criticism from other Southerners. Houston shrugged it off. "Do I have to be wrong too?"

In 1857 the slave states threatened to secede. Houston hurried home to run for governor. He hoped to keep Texas in the Union.

That summer he rode 1500 miles with a plow salesman. They slept out-of-doors. He made forty-seven speeches, some lasting four hours. But the voters chose the other candidate.

He returned to Washington for his last two years as senator. He lost many friends with his fight against secession. Once, someone asked about the unusual vest Houston was wearing. "Is it wildcat or tiger?"

"Neither," replied Houston. "It is leopard. I wear it because the Bible says that the leopard cannot change its spots."

In Congress, he tried to get justice for the Indians and complained that West Point graduates wouldn't recognize a deer track.

He longed to be home with his family. His letters to Margaret were signed, "My love to all. Ever thine, Houston."

*D*uring the next election, one speech was enough to get him elected governor of Texas. In December 1859 he moved his family into the three-year-old governor's mansion in Austin.

After much wrangling, the Texas senate bought furniture, including a seven-foot bed for the new governor. An extra bedroom was created to make room for the lively bunch of children.

Sam Jr., sixteen, attended an academy in Bastrop, but the six others included thirteen-year-old Nannie, eleven-year-old Maggie, nine-year-old Mollie, and seven-year-old Nettie.

Sam Jr. now had a second little brother, William Rogers. Willie was a year old, but it was five-year-old Andrew Jackson who kept everyone busy.

Andrew was allowed to play in one of the offices of the capitol building. One day, he locked the senators in their meeting room and ran home. On the way, he threw the key into a flower bed. Only the threat of going to jail made him tell where it was.

The last child, named Temple Lea for his grandfather, was born at the governor's mansion in the summer of 1860. Afterwards, Margaret was so ill that her husband did not leave her side for ten days.

That year, at the San Jacinto celebration, friends had nominated the sixty-eight-year-old governor for president, but he withdrew. As he predicted, Abraham Lincoln won the election.

That caused South Carolina to secede, and other states followed. Houston believed the Confederacy would fail and tried to keep Texas in the Union. Many called him a traitor.

Some even dared him to show his face. Houston rented the balcony of the Tremont Hotel in Galveston and gave a stinging speech.

Sam Jr. ignored his father's advice and joined the Confederate army. The Texas legislature also ignored the governor. They voted for secession and set March 18, 1861, as the date for every state official to swear an oath of loyalty to the Confederacy.

All night long, Margaret heard her husband pacing the upstairs hall. At daylight he came down. "Margaret," he said, "I will not do it."

That day at noon, the call came, "Sam Houston!" There was no answer. The office of Texas governor was declared vacant and a new governor named.

In the letter he wrote this time, Houston did not resign. Still claiming to be governor, he said, "Fellow citizens, in the name of my own conscience, I refuse to take this oath."

Houston also refused Lincoln's offer of troops to restore his office. He wanted no bloodshed. They hurriedly packed.

As the family started toward Cedar Point, Houston had Jeff turn the small buggy around. They drove to the Treaty Oak on the edge of Austin. Houston paced off the area covered by its spreading branches. He explained how the Indians had used the tree as a gathering place.

Even though the old general didn't agree with secession, he reviewed the troops where Sam Jr. was training in the Confederate army. Margaret, who wrote poetry and hated war, grieved terribly when word came that Sam Jr. had been killed at the battle of Shiloh. In fact, he had been severely wounded.

In September 1862, Lincoln issued the Emancipation Proclamation. The Confederate states ignored this document which freed the slaves. But Houston had such a strong belief in the United States Constitution that he freed his slaves as soon as he heard.

Money became scarce, and the Houston houses were sold. In Huntsville, they rented a house shaped like a steamboat. Houston had dreams of Texas being a republic again.

At the steamboat house, among fig trees

and crepe myrtle bushes, Houston placed his rawhide-bottom chair under a live oak tree. His friends, the nearby Alabama Indians, came to visit. Slowly, his dream for Texas faded away.

In April 1863, Houston set his affairs in order. In large, somewhat shaky letters, he signed his will with the familiar "I am Houston."

On July 26, 1863, his children gathered, and Margaret sat beside his bed reading from the Bible. The old general roused a little and then spoke his last words, "Texas . . . Texas . . . Margaret."

Margaret took from her husband's hand the ring Elizabeth Houston had placed there fifty years before. The children read the word written inside. It said "Honor."

AUTHOR'S NOTE

The man who shaped Texas is buried in Huntsville. The steamboat house and the town house with separate log-cabin law office are open for visitors. The museum in Huntsville contains Houston family items, including Houston's leopard vest and some of the little wooden objects he carved.

Margaret Lea Houston moved to Independence after her husband's death. Four years later, while nursing yellow fever victims, she died. Because of fear of spreading the disease, her wish to be placed beside her husband could not be honored. She is buried in Independence.

Sam Jr. recovered and studied medicine. Nannie acted as mother to the younger children. Maggie became a fine writer, and Nettie was a poet. Mollie ran the post office in Abilene, Texas. Andrew attended West Point, organized a troop of Rough Riders, and for years took care of the San Jacinto battleground. He was a strong advocate of prohibition and women's rights. Willie became an Indian agent. Temple was handsome and flamboyant like his father.

In writing this biography, the author used many sources. One of the most interesting was written from notes made by Jeff Hamilton, the young boy Houston bought that hot afternoon. The Houstons had taught him to read and write. Hamilton, who claimed to be nearly 100 years old, spoke when the historical marker was placed at Cedar Point. He was special guest during the Texas Centennial in 1936 and had his picture taken under the Treaty Oak.

Hamilton's book acknowledges the horror of slavery, but he speaks fondly of Sam Houston. He gives a personal look at the man who shared cookies with him as they rode in the buggy.

Houston slaves were taught a trade and could keep any money they earned. Joshua was a blacksmith and repaired wagons. One day, after the war was over, Joshua rode to Independence with a worn leather bag containing $2000 in gold and American currency. The Houston fortune was gone, and Joshua offered Margaret Houston his life savings. Refusing the gift, she urged him to educate his children. He did so, and they became community leaders.

INDEX

Text set in 14 pt. Times Roman type
with chapter initial letters in 32 pt. Exchequer Script
Illustrations rendered in pencil with overlays
Printed on acid-free recycled paper
Printing and binding by Thomson-Shore